Circles and Curves

Published by the same author

Whipping Hearts Like Gigs
(The Fortune Press, 1954)

Circles and Curves

A Collection of Poetry

Mary Vivian Kernick

Blenheim Press Limited
Codicote

© Mary Vivian Kernick 2010

Mary Kernick has asserted her right
under the Copyright Designs and Patents Act
to be identified as the Author of this work.

Published in 2010
by
Blenheim Press Ltd
Codicote Innovation Centre
St Albans Road
Codicote
Herts SG4 8WH
www.blenheimpressltd.co.uk

ISBN 978-1-906302-19-1

Typeset by TW Typesetting, Plymouth, Devon

Printed and bound in Great Britain by
CPI Antony Rowe, Chippenham and Eastbourne

CONTENTS

Introduction	ix
Where Did She Go, Me?	1
Stampede in Neptune's Stable	2
Young Man – Meet Eve	3
Listen to the Ghosts	4
Wish Who Dares	5
Who Called Misère?	6
To Win	8
To My Cat Philippa	9
Time of My Life	12
Sun and Lovers	14
Secret from the Caves	16
Pop Goes the World	17
Pompey's Progress	19
Peopling the Picture	21
Not Your Move, Man	23
Not Conifer	25
Not a Word	27
My Pet Playboy	28
Murmur of the Innocent	30
Motoring Incident	32
Mind Puzzle	33
Sun-up, People!	34
Mind and I	36
Might and Main	37
Ménage à Deux	39

Love . . .	40
Look Carefully	41
The Life Force	42
Letter to a Man Asleep	43
Let Me Remember	46
In Duplicate	47
Implosion	48
Inhibited Habitats	50
I, Volcano	51
Family Matters	53
Erotica for My Lover	54
Emma's Poem	55
Down to Earth	56
Despair Who Rides	57
Dem Dry Bones	59
The Chatham Funeral, 1951	61
Blood is a Dry Travesty	63
Birth of Spring	64
The Azure Glass-House	65
All the World's a Stage	66
All at Sea (1)	67
All at Sea (2)	69
A Grave Condition	71
We Have Been Robbed, Friends	72
Under the Pine, on the Parquet	74
Having Buried a Precious Embryo Alive	76
The Audit	77
One Into Two Will Go	79
God Knows	80
Torrey Canyon, Ship of Death	81
Proverb	84

Dedication:

    To my friends

'... But I, being poor, have only my dreams;
I have spread my dreams under your feet.
Tread softly because you tread on my dreams.'
W. B. Yeats

INTRODUCTION

These poems are stations along my lifeline; recitations of joy, sorrow and love – and fun.

'Circles and Curves' follows long after my first book of poetry, 'Whipping Hearts Like Gigs', published by Fortune Press in 1954. Those were the stage-whispers and bellows of youth – the word in your ear or the raspberry in your trombone – and with maturity I confess not too much has changed. This book covers both the fruits of age and the middle years. I do not work fast; it is a journey through most of my lifetime.

I have been discreet about the indiscretions but not about the disasters and desires. I wish there was more to relate; so many of the stages were left unrecorded because I was too pressured, too diverted or too despairing to put the words together. Writing poetry is *so hard*.

Of friendship there has been richness beyond measure – a huge and lasting bonus. And there are the rewarding hobbies of working creatively in silver to make jewellery and designing clothes.

But now, I have lost my three cats, Delilah, Jomo and Pompey, and this is a sadness. I have never been alone if there was a cat in the room, so have now 'rescued' Pluto, a gorgeous tabby.

WHERE DID SHE GO, ME?

Where did she go, me?
I'd started to bear her impression so lightly
That I didn't notice her leave.
I've searched my world for a clue
But she's become a foreigner
On another level,
A cosmic casualty.
Potions or therapies
Could have sent her
Away with the fairies,
She might have been subsumed
(But by what or whom?)
Or tossed from post to pillar,
My familiar.
Still wearing her transparency,
I can screen her performance
On my retinas in absentia.
There is an occasional reference
When I wake up in her sleep,
A knowing gesture,
But no solid matter.
Where were we
When I parted you from us?

STAMPEDE IN NEPTUNE'S STABLE

On this menacing morning
Hearing each moment
Hoof-beats more insistent and compelling,
Seeing these sleek playboy ponies swelling
Up to stallions and bucking
The bird riders on their wild white flanks
Beneath other breasting broncos
Breaking their ranks
And – bits sawing through slavering lips
That spume at heaven –
Still more galloping epileptics
Belling and skidding
Into this contagious fit,
Defying quietus . . .

On this menacing morning
Waiting each moment
For rockets bursting
Over lifeboat launching
By woken sleepers,
Because some vessel fishing
Has been trampled over
And lies on its face . . .

On this menacing morning
We can only hope the rescuer,
Its reins in its teeth
And its belly full of Trojans
(Those galvanised dreamers)
Was called for Pegasus.

YOUNG MAN – MEET EVE

Young man – meet Eve, the automaton.
Yes, her decorative face looks real
Eyes asparkle, lips apart
Above draped limbs in subtle motion,
And the playful palms that fondle
Softening up your heartfelt mind
Seem kind,
Until your harp of tongue begins,
Plucked by her dart,
To plead for plight of peak of boon
A summit deed, a union.

Unmasking instantly
The turned temptress
Bares her steel spine,
Dissembling knuckles cinch and whine –
As the outraged flirt
Too she is mechanically expert,
As provocateur lethal.
Love, floored,
Measures a grave along its route
And spits before it dies
At the puppet with bright glass eyes
Straddling Venus's boot.

Young man met Eve:
No Eden, no apple, no idyll.
Day done, in downing dark he wept
And slept alone,
A novice still.

LISTEN TO THE GHOSTS

Listen, the ghosts are talking
As they emanate and elongate at midnight;
Shrugged into empty robes
They are walking the house.
There are hosts of them
Jumbled and bundled
Who separate sweetly,
Neatly like stamps,
When people walk through them;
Nothing is torn or bruised
While they're stalking the rooms in the dark.
Gathered under their umber wraps
At witching hours
And undeterred by sharp quoins or electric flares,
Imperceptibly, still whispering,
They proceed to their conclusions
And fold away.
If you're passing them,
Listen to the ghosts,
Clarify their murmurs as best you can.
Knowing that one day
You will join them
Process what they say punctiliously,
Hear them and listen,
The ghosts are talking.

WISH WHO DARES

Do you wish on the small forked bone,
Still damp when handy,
Articulating by stentorian or sibilant means
Your liking?
Wishes can be deviant
Or seductive schemes
But the furcula itself is not choosy,
Simply a device
To opt for token trivia
Or infinitely complex dreams,
(Absurd heroics maybe).
Anyone can perform this painless pantomime
And break its wings
Without inducing screams.
But, for the robbed bird,
It's key.

WHO CALLED MISÈRE?

Heart you have woken!
Didn't we have a deal,
Whereby you dozed on through my waking
Wrapped in my flesh,
Seeking no stimulus if I gave lodging
And aired your bed with zephyrs
Whilst you slept?
You had your quiet life
And I all the painless gaiety I needed
For when I rode roughshod over suits of hearts
In games of chance
You were well-cushioned, weren't you,
Against any glancing knave?
And when it came your turn to romance
The odds were that it would be a walkover
Because all your games were fixed.
Heart, I always covered you.

So I kept my part,
Never let a soul know you,
You were a stranger even to me:
A clock ticking in a sealed room
Whose comforting momentum
Was the thief of time.
And you encouraged me to be daring
On my Cinderella evenings
So long as I returned unchaperoned –
Many's the glass slipper I left in ballrooms
To shatter on the midnight chime.

But some deft hand has dazzled you –
A suit unsignalled,
And instead of biding quietly behind my ribs
You quicken suddenly and jolt my fist.
Now I have been tricked and hearts are trumps!
Not diamond-hard nor sharp as club or spade
But raw and ripe and needy,
Never to be assuaged
Until blood turns to water
Down the long arteries and threads the veins
To flood your chambers in old age.

Heart, you are throbbing
And will not let me curl around you to sleep
For all my inducements.
If I could live to do it I would claw you out
And let your room to a yeti or a recluse
Rather than have this distracted organ inhabit.
Meantime you expose us like the bearded lady
Or the choleric dwarf to ribald wit.
Growth in my side,
The world has other vignettes to study –
Let us hide – have mercy –
No more tricks !

TO WIN

Not knowing how
The rotor drives the shaft
That cranks the plane or plough,
Nor why
Loose earth spins on its poles
And yet cleaves whole,
What stuff myrrh is
Or ectoplasm,
Being barely elite
And fairly prayer-less:
If you can sense
The thrust at the tip of a root,
The quick at the start of a life,
Not cumbered by lazy ways
But supple innately,
If you practise living
Not just process the notes and theory
Then you, the green outsider
In the human obstacle race,
Will overtake the favoured runners –
Those promoted with spin
And emblazoned in colours –
And you will win!

TO MY CAT PHILIPPA

O you've such bright eyes my luvvy
When I hold you tight in my cradle arms;
Only you'll not stay,
You'll spurt away
Or claw and spar
Philippa!
What a wild child you are,
A chintzy little miss
With glist'ning fur,
Red hairs on your heaped up back like a fire
(I can see you're listening ...).
You're a fast girl too
With your toms touting
At the back and front door,
A proper young lady
Sitting beneath the bushes
Aloof and apart
But an outrageous dare
In the flare of your eyes
From your little flame heart.
Such a squeezable miss,
Sleek ears in the air,
Opening the door
With swing of hips
And flare of tail,
Gauging the uttermost comfortable,
Ample and amiable
Lap on which to fix;
Or perhaps a parade along the sill
If there's an audience climbing the hill

Who look liable
To admire you to your full.
Even after surgery
You wore the bandage at a chic angle
Like a tea-gown by Dior
Or a crisp cotton,
And studied your image in the window.

For a moment you lie with me
Fluffy and puffy
Then you're off, huffy –
'that's enough of that!'
I hereby will and declare you
Heir to my estate and money
If you outlive me
And I leave any.
There shall be purchased by my executor
A haircomb and a brush
Of tortoiseshell and silver,
Claw-file and pedicure,
Powdered fish talcum
With a halibut perfume,
Baths of thick milk
And a rinse to embellish your fur,
Collars of ribbons,
Eiderdowns
And a little electric blanket,
Twenty pairs of earrings hung on hooks
For you to slap and abandon
And forty tins of Cornish cream
To grease your purr,
Cheesy mice for dreams of birds,

Bacon rinds, crisp cornflakes with curds,
Filleted fish and jellied eel,
A cat-proof watch with a pretty tock-tick,
Drops of Cadbury's milk chocolate
And a toffee-apple on a stick;
And all because I adore you more
Than cats can know or cats could care Philippa.
Purr, Philippa . . .
O you've such bright eyes my buzzy
And I'll stroke you now, it's a pleasure –
Don't meow!

TIME OF MY LIFE

Turn the timer over
And flow sand slowly
To re-run this history
Grain by single grain,
Blip by blip.
For introduction let's recall
Being shaken half to death
While queuing for entry
To the birth canal
And then, when still unready,
Sent through on a dry run –
A mere handful of matter –
And almost lost.
No wonder I sometimes strayed later
Too near the edge of the world
And stumbled through decades.
In the scramble upward
Sap was scattered
And spillages occurred –
But I could still skim shooting stars
Through firmaments of heavenly bodies
And watch them skitter across the sky
On good days.
Then there were the set performances –
Fireworks for the over-forties –
In a show of rude strength.
Both bone hips replaced
By cinched fists
Which remain on their mettle;
A hearty pacemaker

Squires me wherever I go.
Betimes life was a tussle,
A lover shrunk somewhere
Inside a disembodied voice,
Anxiety acute
Though therapeutically contained.
But fight the fight, girl!
Now you have learnt how to battle without rancour
The atmosphere has cooled
And skirmishing is child's play.
And no, it won't be necessary
To swap birthday-suit for chain mail
When you go naked into the tournament finally –
What fun that day!

SUN AND LOVERS

Sun up there!
Slithering jellyfish on top of the air
Oozing yourself along inch by inch
Your stinging belly bare:
Keep your distance.

Brilliant emperor treading ether
Stay out of reach:
You, ablaze in your element,
Exposing the minions beneath
To that fiery breath.

Lord-High-Swordfish,
Your blades part the dry ocean
To impale those bodies laid out on sand sheets –
Haul back your diving hun
Brandishing iron, you sadist!

Ruthlessly stingray-king
Your shaft strikes home,
Piercing the serried ranks of flesh and bone.
But, instead of carrion,
Behold all those plumped skeletons
splendid in skin-tight gold.

They angled for you, sunfish,
Drew you down
And called your broiling bluff,
Who now levitate in their pleasure
At the singular ardour

Of your love,
For Neptune by comparison's a chiller
And earth – no sinuous Romeo –
Will lie above them long enough.

SECRET FROM THE CAVES

Secret from the caves of night
We roll the boulders back like balls,
Like globes of mercury,
And send our bodies forth
Over the quick-silver threshold
To a world where we discreet pedestrians
Transport ourselves.
Reflecting each other's
Your eyes are emerald, mine amber,
Our subtle contours nippled with opals
And faces medals on the plush dark.
Sloughing away our public skin
Has transfigured each feature
So that no stumbling intruder knows us
(And even if told would say
'They are not themselves.')
You who see only our flat dull daytime identities
Look! these are the real people.
We who plead other proprieties,
Lack bravura to stay
And hold up our full facets to the dazzle day –
Who cannot bear light on our jewellery,
We it is who belie.
Look away.

POP GOES THE WORLD

This may be the last dance ...
Waltz away sophisticated bodies
Orbiting the alcoves of memory;
Go back to the gauche steps
That straddled the edges of your nursery
And its one small light
Flickering like a spectrola
On the walls of a darkened Lyceum.
Then the wages of sin
Were pocket income
And every young body was brave
In the brazen face of a pop-gun.
So search again the cute pictures
On the hard cardboard pages;
Be slow to outgrow
The scene so secure and simpatico
As you pirouette
Over the polished ballroom
Dressed up like men and women.
Don't go full circle –
Come back people!
This may be the last dance ...

Remember to tunes
In your garden of happiness,
To a brown bird singing his songs of love,
Or muse under spreading chestnut
On the world's fine romance
Before smoke gets in your eyes.
Why does my heart go boom

During the entr'acte, the terrace idyll
With your Daisy Bell?
You need only recall
Just one of those foolish things
To be diverted.
Surely you don't want to set the world on fire?
Slow down!
Don't crush your honeysuckle rose
Against the closing bars of the beguine.

Yet who can stop you –
You with a flame in your heart –
Asking the only girl in the world
For the last dance?
No! go now
Back to your Sorrento
Or this will be the last chance
To step it at all lightly
Before your lithe legs crumple and fall
Under your swaying back –
Because, perfidia,
Every random flimsy body
Will be blown up and burst
After the ball.

POMPEY'S PROGRESS

A puss unbooted and undressed,
Near naked skin sucked raw
And blotched with pigment.
Not a figment, cat Pompey, of anybody's dream
Nor a delusion in the eye of the beholder,
For it had become quite clear:
Here we had inexplicable baldness.
There were diagnoses, references to neuroses,
Hyper-activity, immune deficiency,
Traumatic stress and other scenes.
He became a testers' pin-cushion,
Needle, swab, diet, pill;
No deficit of expense or attention
From veterinarians orthodox and homeopathic
Of indubitable skill.
One last throw by owner
(Now pulling out own hair):
A healer was summoned.
And, with God and medium interposed
Somewhere between the animal and his condition,
The bald tide turned.
He was healed over short weeks
By the light laying on of hands.
Might the headline go:
'Feline Cured by Human Faith'?
Because the cat had no input as far as I know.
Many sympathisers and doubting Toms
Inspected the regrowth, which was total,
A soft splendent mantle.
A bolt from heaven

Or just from yonder
Out of the agnostic blue?
Acceptable whichever
As a small miracle,
Owner content.
The cat, of course, never knew he was unkempt
And had quite forgotten
His fleeting awareness of wondrous things.

PEOPLING THE PICTURE

Gauge a full breast of canvas sky –
That's starting from the top,
Prop it up on hedges and trees
Above fields in full grass skirts
Edged with small stones,
Cream in aquamarine tones
On the starboard side
Capping with smidgeons of froth,
Then in foreground down to the feet, sand.

Cliques on the strand;
An unauthorised deputation cheeping about expenses,
Chewing over living-costs;
The webbed-ones' caucus flaps
And the boss bird gives them a bit of beak
And tells them to move back.
One apart, of independent opinions,
Probes his wings and cleans his preened chest,
Muttering malevolently on a dais of granite.
Great bronzed beauty man
Is studying his ripe reflection
But, when the tidal mirror breaks and flattens,
Flinches from the fall-out;
He too swells his furred chest but leaves it at that.
A thick-thighed bucket of a child
Has coaxed the coterie to draw near
And then dismissed it with a brick.
Later parliament reassembles,
Cawing to the gallery and dropping missiles
Of tinder-dry bread.

Then it seems the order is 'bale out' –
Save your feathers – jettison all freight –
Only ingest sufficient fuel for the route.
Later on, a single gull
Rubs one leg up against the other
And devours every crumb.

NOT YOUR MOVE, MAN

Having triggered creation
God, the Grand-Master,
Flexed His fingers over His galaxial board
And steadied the pieces as they spun by,
Sliding them about the sky
In chequered symmetry
Through four days to proverbial writ;
Then stood back,
Balanced their interactive movements,
Embellished them
And rested.

Each piece of original shrapnel
(Honed on time's friction
And disciplined by its function
In the zodiac)
Gave a meteoric display,
But man's concern is the one globoid bolt
From which he started on the sixth day
In all his nubile promise.

Since then our earth has moved and spun
With such precision about the sun
And still she stars in the galaxy,
But her looks belie:
We have blazed her no planetary trails
To vie with Saturn,
Only white farts of explosion
And mushroom puffs,
Minutely impudent and unsavoury.

Mankind has not moved well
But perhaps the master's purposes were playful,
We merely chessmen
Whose black v. white hostilities are at His whim
Not of our making.
Bishops can act deviously like knights,
Castles are razed in crooked games
And unempowered people
Are held in pawn by terrorists
In their Messiahs' names –
Stealing a move on the devil
Whose gamesmanship's unchecked.

Best blame man's two folk-heroes, haloed and horned,
For all our quick and deadly theses
Before the crump of holocaust smashes the pieces.

NOT CONIFER

On a cross
On a cairn
On a mound
It hung, it swayed,
One gaudy bauble
All spangle and sparkle
Above the unmade plot.
A rubber-duck
Would not have seemed
So incongruous on that cross,
So quaint a tableau.

At the next burial
It was flashy still,
Bothering mourners' eyes
Like a loose lash
Or SOS from limbo.
To those distracted people
A halo'd ghost
Swinging from the gibbet
Would have been more credible,
But it was not that.

On a cairn
On a mound
A cross with one bauble
Dangling from the boom.
How contrary!
Pagan pennant on holy mast
And answerable to whom?

But strip not the dead man's Christmas tree
In the cemetery of his hope
Which is dreary enough, surely,
And where in the New Year
He will R.I.P. ad nauseam,
Pared by minikin teeth to bone
Beneath his marble blurb.

NOT A WORD

There is nothing left to say,
No word wide enough to convey
A soundless void
Nor, through this dumb excess,
Could the sharpest sound pick a way.
And when all is done
I have only asked for a few spun notes from my pen
I have only wanted the way of them to go down,
But here in the paper there is a great raw cleft
And there are just no syllables to fill
The nothing that is left.

MY PET PLAYBOY

Sitting on the throne watching me shower
To the hum of his low baritone
Jomo relishes his happy-hour,
With brisk massage and then breakfast
(A rich repast to prime his day).
After which,
His coat groomed to dressage sheen,
He departs for business in some lush boardroom,
With filtered lighting and a green address.
Back later, still in mellow mien
And murmuring cryptic snippets about where he's been,
He'll nestle closer, deign to adore,
To ogle, to paw,
With eyes like sooty diamonds
Soliciting my pleasure.
Then a wash, before pulling down
The covers over the day-bed
And nesting.
Occasionally requesting
The prerogative to supervene
In small domestic matters,
To signal his wishes, order treats.
Otherwise disarmingly serene,
Affable to guests.
Tough-guy rarely,
Only when required to comply
With quite unreasonable requests –
'Will you stop it?' or 'Move please!'
Then he may respond
With a fisticuff or gruff expletive,

Mild mayhem and soon done.
But, rising promptly at 4am,
Leaving the warm duvet
Out my lion strides – chocks away –
To rove his kingdom,
Have dominion over
The whiskered minions who quake and quiver
Inside their furry socks.
For Jomo Jekyll has slipped his lead
And become the hun, demon of the Grove.
Never coy – I'm told he's as brutal,
My pet playboy,
As Genghis Khan or Ivan the Terrible
When he's stalking for prey
On his beat.

MURMUR OF THE INNOCENT

People! Lend us your hands
To feel for a flickering pulse
In this building's bowel,
Entombed in its gut.
A living doll
Has plunged down the chute
From an anonymous apartment
To inhabit these wastelands.

Forward! disposal squads
With gloves and bins
Hoping for diamonds in the garbage –
Cold and pricey and hard –
Or other profitable discharge

You have arrived mercifully, starless kings,
For a child has been delivered
On a soiled litter
Again to shame the world:
Put down your sacks, empty of gifts,
And push your searching arms
Into the rodents' manger.

There to uncover
In that sump of hell,
Still slurred with baptismal dottle,
A murmuring heart in its birthday parcel,
Soft and non-negotiable.

Witness!
Witness the atrocity
Visited upon a daughter
Denied before cock-crow
Every griping morning
Every sullen twilight
Then born to murderers.

Dustmen, recover her –
We should tip them with frankincense and myrrh –
Before our generic soul,
With God's good-riddance,
Is sucked into the quagmire
Of a global septic tank.

MOTORING INCIDENT

Out of my mind it grew
Revving its way
Round the bend of pain
With screams of rubber,
Mapless and blind
Like a demented ball.

We motored through,
Mind and I,
To peaceful heydays
But we will always wear
Subtly, like a flinch of gossamer,
A reminder of how it was
When hell was on wheels
And we under.

MIND PUZZLE

The puzzle pieces lie in little dumps.
Not scattered, more imploded into
Or erupted from
And still twitching.
Each one expresses
Not just its own ache
But all the might-have-been scenarios
Waiting on its completion:
This could have been a coruscating vision
Or tragi-comic,
But it's now all history and dust
After the boggled mind bust
And broke up.

SUN-UP, PEOPLE!

Lie there, lucky ones,
Speared on ignipotent rays
By brands of sun,
Downing trapped beams
Through pores in burnished skins
And burying them in your shady byways.

Swarm on them, Excellency,
Whoever they are, while they grovel in sand
Or float on sea
For diathermy.
There is more in this world than bean to ripen
And foetus to expand,
There are those winter minds with icy hands,
Gripped bodies blocked and battened
Like Pluto's seeds;
Those who may never sublimate par,
Rev up to a wrought passion or
A star's stint of motion
– Oracular
– Eureka!

So whoever you are
Who open below to the King,
Open heart, open mind,
Open swaddling!
Let this light-giver pierce you
Like a consummation.
The primal sun

Wrap close to breast and bind
To soul and seal,
The teeming one
The headlong benefaction.

MIND AND I

We're back from the brink,
In-the-pink,
No crude kidding!
It's all over with the shouting –
We wouldn't want to leave you
Possibly doubting
The outcome.
We are found well and happy,
So lucky,
Challenging and winning and enjoying,
Positing success
Naught less.

MIGHT AND MAIN

Sea tenderly
Bathes the extremities of land's body
In a foaming shampoo,
Effaces the grime and sweat with solicitous fingers
And polishes with liquid chiffon.
Only notice when she sinks back wearily
How those limpid hands turn blue.

It might be a neon signal!
Instantly the vegetation –
All pampered upon the flesh of the land,
All pollen and seed –
Tosses its hydra-heads,
Scattering scurf and sand in insolent mien
Over those buffed extremities
So lately clean.
But once too often:
Sea's deepening brow furrow upon furrow
Darkens with storm,
Transforms her anointing force into an enemy
Advancing and assaulting with her own unarmed body,
Getting up off obeisant knees torn ragged and bloody
And hurling her gauge at a cloud.
Then the blacked eye of the sky flows;
The nattery teasel,
Dandelion with falling hair,
Sapling, seedling, vegetable, vine,
Rampant or rare,
Hump their backs over folded shoulders, intertwine,

As crops that, capering pertly,
Are slewed like a drunk corps de ballet by bullying air.

But reprieve.
The once-wail of the sea hushed and sighing,
Over the wet land silently
Each piskey shelters under his leaf
And the lady with lucent limbs returns,
Remorsefully retracing,
Soothing this rock-taut face, that gape of chine,
Soaking land's corns and calluses
And all her sore appendages in brine.

Adversary each and lover,
Currently at issue but tided together
In constant liaison:
So bog to bedrock
Shale to alluvion
Clinch and shrink in infinity's gridlock
As always and from now on.

MÉNAGE À DEUX

I told her to go – 'Just go!' I said,
For suddenly I'd sussed her,
This Jezebel to my Juliet.
Our dwelling was hell's cellar
Until the penetrating sun,
Nature's chandelier, switched on
And I could see
She was only the shadow of me.
Now we can be ourself
And celebrate my duality in person
One to one.

LOVE . . .

It is important for you to love me.
How much can you spare?
Because I need to be loved
And it needs to be true,
Do not simulate or manufacture
Or josh along for the ride –
I shall know!
I need love like a tourniquet
For the permanent wound of my birth,
A survival measure
Not a cute girdle to wear.
I've been seen to court it,
Cajole, coquet,
Adulate even,
But do not expect me to return it
Because on my part
It was sleight of heart,
There is nothing there.

LOOK CAREFULLY

Throw back your blinds, eyes!
Veiled in purdah,
Shuttered windows on oriel sills;
Refill both lamps,
Burnish both rosebowls.
Now the sun's hot breath
Is flushing their bays
It is time for your lidded oracles
To dance and quicken.
– But carefully,
For if you cannot loose their latch
And force the panes
The cords will tear
And the sash snap back,
Uncovering – beware!
Not lash-hung irises
Beautiful and rare
But blind spots, marbles,
Lolling inanely,
Crystallised gristle.

THE LIFE FORCE

Bucking the dictation
Of learned constraints
A pulse inside the body
Gathers impetus –
Awaits the Romeo with art
To prise apart ribs
Picketing the vital organ.
Catching an arterial bus
He will snatch the wheel
And, from a jumped start,
Rip the gears through to top,
A racing cert.
Then blood will follow,
Gird its long skirts
And roar down chasms,
Regroup, re-engage
Every curd of clot
Of nature's ruby wage;
Arteries are sagged and bagged
Where the bore pressed,
Yet hyper-resilient
At its summation.

So reams of pages runed in red
Run streaming with their story
Through this self this id this one
And on and on,
For we are only carriers of heredity
And after we've strewn our pollen on our hours
With the subtle sexual rub of a bee on flowers
The flood will drown us.

LETTER TO A MAN ASLEEP

Dear Roberto Shuteyevitch
Or Red River Robert,
I won't wake you up –
I'm too lazy, not crazy enough
To circumnavigate the snores
And rouse a sonorous corpse.
No hopes to coax
A coffee-cup here
Where nobody knocks before one o'clock
On the nattery letterbox.
Better Robert should snore
Pallid and pure
Than bristle-up and roar
Unpleasant plenties
Through the jittery box in the door.
Behind it picture
Paintings abstracted,
Mobiles in spate
And framed-up blizzards of colour enacted
In oils on the walls
Till he wakes again
And coins some more
Reliefs for the spaces,
Between their embraces,
The nude naked reaches
The speckly speeches
Of walls.
Then they'll all be warm
In the icy dawn –
Well-packed they can pinch out

Jack Frost from each other
And smother a holing yawn.
There'll be cafe au lait
In the cafe today
While he scrubs up the platters
And discards and scatters
The offcuts and tatters,
All to boost his exchequer
And fulfil the demands
Of his landlilord. –
So to his kitchen, welcome,
All labouring tenants
And itchy skivers
But couturiers spurious
And bankers curious
Out, out!
Or in the whim of his mood
He'll lay about you
Rout you
With washing-up cloth clout you
And call you thieves of his time.
Spurning his Horlicks
For the visions that wait upon scouring of plates.
The muse works late
And the painter wakes not
At half-past eight
Brush in hand
Paint in eye
Soul in spate;
He staggers up late
On any old date
And woe betide they

Who startle the gingerly play
Of sleep from his whiskery cheek
Or lace his turps.
A peg off a sock
A sock off a line
To stuff in the clattery mouth of the box.
Cat, stop your backchat !
You'll lick off your spats
Before Robert will waken
You Tom.
Forsaken forsaken
Beard of Brennan
Sleep on,
We're gone.

LET ME REMEMBER

Let me remember the born-demented
Born-beggared and born-stunted
Lurching across the shrinking continents
Of this one world
And the sane, bonny dead.

Let me not in formaldehyde
Preserve a jello ghost
And exhibit it around
Bottled up in my transparent mind
To buy hard-luck.

But let me mourn, O lovers O mothers,
Whilst you reflect my loss;
It left so faint a print
Within its sanctum
And yet the emotional quick is pricked and porous.

So let me mollify my sorrow,
Time's drift will temper it
To this one world
But the hole now in my Caucasian shell
Is black as Calcutta's
And would make of me a mausoleum.

IN DUPLICATE

Through drizzle and dark
In the night's brain
A moist moon slides
By my windowpane
Between the fluted drapes;
A single moon
On the wax and the wane,
Now two moons
One with spry legs dancing
One bald-head laughing,
Slick as spoons;
Two moons slide
To the edge of the pane,
Siamese-moons,
One moon again,
One moon cagged
On the ledge of the frame.
Gone moon, moons,
Into the curtain,
Not a lick left or trail on the pane
Phantom or phosphor;
Two glazed sheets
Stare square-eyed
Through the rain –
Blindly into ether.
So who could blame
Their lonely eyes
For making a toy each
From the sky's
Solitary aside?

IMPLOSION

When the world goes bang –
Blows up in guts and grit
In Methuselah's clock and disfigures it
Tearing him limb from face –
There'll be no alarums,
Only the silent sand-man
Come to smother his screech
With a blanket of dust.

For when all's done
What reverence have we shown
For Time's immaculate litany
Of centenaries and seasonal turns,
For dating and placing us
And meting out our spans?
– To be maligned into the bargain
As thief, as cheat, as enemy,
A thrifty old clone
Who gets his January in his December's belly.

Those hands once set so straight
Will scratch his dial,
Dysfunctional claws
Cagging the punctilious cogs of his measure,
While with movement unbalanced –
No spring in the gait –
He trips up every digit on his beat.
Pointless to decry his clarion conscience
When his works are stricken
And nearly every tock's been ticked;

No cause to curse his zealotry
Now that the alarming breath has gone from his lung.

Thus with our sentinel grandfather struck dumb
(Stunned by his own pendulum)
You could steal Time's gems on a whim,
But the jewels are redundant
When no watchmakers are clocking on,
No point then in time and motion
Or cosmic flashbacks to the year one.

Seeing this floundering automaton
Barking his bobbin on every shin
As it unwinds to oblivion
We'll be helpless to save him.
And just for an instant of himself
When we've torn his hands from his disfigurement
He will see the advantage taken
By innumerable conmen
Who have wound him on.

Likewise too late, watchmen, watchwomen,
To fill in blank diaries
Or observe anniversaries
Beside swaying cenotaphs over the planet,
To indict the deadly quick
And the quickly dead commemorate
In one composite recall.
Time's total calendar in a billion scraps –
Spilled centuries, momentous fragments,
Broken dates – all
Littering the infinity of space.

INHIBITED HABITATS

They holed up in parched oases
Boldly posturing
Gestures and grimaces
From a podium of space:
They think they're safe.

Since the sanctum of my birth
I've been fixing up a nest
With lung-to-lung effect
As cosy as the first
I think I'm safe.

She inside her boudoir
Traps her mind in her make-over
And inhibits its ways
By limiting the brainwaves:
She thinks she's safe.

He has built a screen of speech
And sub-edited it severely
So that no one may discover
It covers a breach:
He thinks he's safe.

You seek nothing for hereafter
Have not hide nor private cloister
Nor closure for your doubt
Yet manifestly feel
You're as safe as a house!

I, VOLCANO

I, volcano,
A glory-hole
With the germ of life
Clenched in its belly,
Ferment in sympathy.

With a fire of blood
And a bowel of mud
And a febrile centre
Grumble in brotherhood.

Slowly in the equinox
We ripen upwards,
A containable organism
Mewling in our system,
Ambitious and irksome.

So when for the cuckoo,
And blithely,
Summer is icumen in
We under a broiling sun
React extravagantly
To its hot breath.

Thus by our autumns,
Retching and labouring,
We've delivered effusions on a volley of wind
Before they are set,
Molten on the world's back
Scarring and scathing.

After much controversy the law may say
We were not causally responsible,
May set aside our ill-wills,
Ignore their specious codicils
When we are dead as dodos ......
Only you, volcano, will be feigning.

Mankind will not endure to see
You the survivor finally
With your eye put out
Go down in smoke;
Nor when every glint's gone dark
From fire to moon,
Jove in Olympia impassively
Cracking the knackered universe with a spoon.

FAMILY MATTERS

One day my mother
Took a ferry over the Styx to a new land
Where, startled, she discovered 'her' waiting,
Indicating the silent toddler on her hand.
Later when a boy joined them,
In haste from life,
Her grand-family was complete.
There she brought up these dead children,
Grew them on,
Shadowing their reluctant mother
Who had been rid of one
And involuntarily shed the other.
Heaven alone knows
What would have become of them
If granny had not stood in,
Come so opportunely to help Him,
The guardian of souls.

And how I wonder will they receive me,
Beloved daughter, benighted mother,
When I shake off my burning ashes
And make for this place,
Parting the celestial ether in search of strangers?
Or will St Peter,
Such a scrupulous shepherd,
Thrice deny me space?

EROTICA FOR MY LOVER

Lover come love like water,
Muscular and tidal,
Heaving itself in waves upon the sand
With irreversible compulsion
Though generous and open-armed.

Lover come love like the bee
Dipping into a flower
Stealthily for honey,
Nosing its way
Plumbing for nectar
Further and further.

Lover come love like lightning
Stabbing and flooring,
Come subtle as poured oil to vessel,
Be as knuckle to the glove
Be as pith to the peel.

Come love as my lover
And as none other,
Eye to known eye
Unwaveringly intimate,
Come tangibly to inhabit.
Having arms and loins about us,
Tongues and ears
Nodes and peninsulas
In endless permutation,
We shall plead more eloquently far
Than prayer, petition or importunate poses
To Eros for eternity on a bed of roses
In flagrante delicto.

EMMA'S POEM

I wish I could have wrapped you in a poem.
I would have said, 'Emma, wear this;
It's flimsy but will retain a subtle imprint of your beauty.
I have spread it quickly as a verse to cushion you
From those harsh wheels.

For instant cover
These threadbare rags of words are all that I can spread;
Everything you have earned and taken with you
Is so much our loss
And more than I can say.

But as I turn, lost and bleakly,
Your gemstone heart's skyhigh
Swelling in greeting and set in brilliants!'
The wisp of poetry drifts away,
Emma is with us still.

DOWN TO EARTH

Falling Eden falling
From the first lair
Rare and phantom
Air oh air
Calling 'Falling fair
Falling fair
Foothold failing
Where baling where?'

Far the earth
The strata'd stone
Unyielding scene
Of cruel coming
Barking bone

But the nuclear soul
Ungrown unknown
Then crawls from its caul
Rearing sheer and tall
Himself his own

DESPAIR WHO RIDES

Despair who rides on my shoulder
Insinuates its leery feelers down
Across the breastbone
And, at a point along the smooth channel
Between my two mites,
Plunges in.

Despair who rides in my lungs
Bores through their stored sighs upward;
A knotted snake aiming for the throat
Until, one hard upon the other,
Its lumps throttle
And its slimy convolutions choke.

Despair who rides inside my eyes
Has spurs that prick from laughter
Tears sudden as storms;
Blundering on
It cuts into the irises with horseshoes
And crazes their egg-white beds.

Despair who rides is my passenger
As much as master and travels free,
It is my prerogative to brake suddenly
And lurch its animal bulk into oblivion . . .
But when these muscles slacken
The monkey is still up on its perch.

Despair who rides me
Unseat yourself – why not? – as wilfully
As the transparency that tenanted my body,
I would lose you even in that way

(It was too easy)
So you leave off mourning.

I will walk behind I swear
At a fair distance for ever
But – for fear,
Wearing that small miracle on my sleeve
I over-balance and topple into a grave –
Ride off me,
Despair who rides.

DEM DRY BONES

Wanton witchdoctor,
Herbalist or manipulator,
Incisor, spiritualist:
Who is there left to treat us
When these perilous times
Strip us from their spindle
Into earth's polluted lap?
Where the balm?

Vegetable curd, animal fat,
Ball-bearing mineral –
Not a lubricant's left unsung
By some millionaire's promoter
For greasing of palms.

Mating dispenses its own physic,
Secretes the most expedient and discreet of oils
In the involuntary product of its toils;
And there's emulsion for troubled water,
Grease-gun for the motor
And blubber for the swimmer in dire straits.

Nevertheless, in spite of our mothers
Administering lotions and warm embrocations,
We've reached our parched majority on tenterhooks,
Knowing there's no patent cure
Nor diversionary measure to deflect our future.

So man will become a touch-paper
For the final provocateur to ignite –
Wild heat will fuse his spinal cord
And char him to the wick

And there will be no laxative for his gut
Nor emollient for the raw quick after exposure.

Fled up a gum-tree,
Stuck to his last post
Screaming for soap or jelly
Or lardy substitute
To soothe his genitals,
His seed will be denied every unction –
Too late to save the children
When their blueprint is erased
From his primary function
And he grilled to his ghost.

THE CHATHAM FUNERAL, 1951

Across the lonely cathedral floor
I can see them,
The little dead boys still human
As they wait out the ceremony
And pivot at the door
For a last look
Before their journey.
Surprised – they are not expecting
Sentries to guard
The likenesses of the boys they were,
The little dead bodies
Of lads for all seasons.
They do not suffer now
The torn flesh smarting
Beneath their patriotic palls,
Nor comprehend the carnage
Which enshrined that happenstance.
They cannot go there
Seeking reasons.

We might have sent the sentries out earlier
To man the route to the barracks
But we weren't aware;
We do our homework in ink not blood,
Not thinking to play our lessons out
By casting the living
In wincing scenes.
And it is also written
That for their sins
Hapless men will still draw lots to drive

The buses that will show us
What little boys are made of
Under their skins.

BLOOD IS A DRY TRAVESTY

Blood is a dry travesty of liquid,
A caustic lucifer
(Water it down, warn,
Water it down);
Blood is a chafing flame that licks the veins
And picks the locks,
It shocks, it devours.

Body is a furnace not to be much stoked,
Blood is a power not to be provoked,
Its bubbling point is low
And the human oasis where it has brothed
And been aglow is unleafed,
Bone is fissured by the heat
And the mind's lens is blown.

Blood is a tide,
Plethora in the side
Which, boiling high,
Whistles no warnings through its circuitry
And one day will burst abreast.
Smashing the heart fount
It will plunge down its flue like a plumb,
Side-step death, burial and everlasting rest
And go to ground
Where, merged with alluvial arteries of earth,
It will help the fecund clay
Promote renewal and rebirth
And be immortalised in that equation.

BIRTH OF SPRING

Observe the staunch green shoots
So newly nascent
And come-lately;
They could codify infinity
Or falter in frost;
Eager enough to commingle
Into a verdant tide
Massing over earth,
Or they might die in a mean dearth.
This is a map of primal growth
And mimics the origin of its species,
It is emerald manna for age and youth
And should grow into a hardy giant,
It is the nub of life
Strong and couth.

THE AZURE GLASS-HOUSE

For me this is nearly all;
Almost nothing else
Beyond here than the beach
And sprawling images
Under the command of gulls,
Turning bodies
With profiles and moods
In an all but perfect globe.

This is practically aloneness
Yet almost all society,
Nine-tenths repletion
And all but bliss.
Only one iota is missing:
The nous to wind this timid ticker
And set its time-bomb off.
So the moon-blue bowl,
All but perfect,
Must be violated
To let one-tenth of a poor fish live.

ALL THE WORLD'S A STAGE

It's not really so strange
That characters cast
With a dip in the mind
Find that the moon just fits it.
Bodies are manned
By impulses and messages
We cannot touch –
Meant to direct us
They flash back and mutiny,
Treacherous, teasy,
No respecters.
So the invert, the loon,
Is dissentient whether
In a class unschooled
A play uncast
Or hive lazy
And by all those standards indubitably phased.
But, whether a knock
From his God or his bike
Deranged the letters in his book of brain,
If we could see the incredible chaos on the page
We would applaud his act,
A part being faithfully,
Meticulously portrayed.

ALL AT SEA (1)

Notice this dolly autumnal lady,
This girlish tableau buoyed and watchful
On crests of pillow.
Her eyes firing a blank of welcome
Up from that comfortable deck
And lips posed for salute
Greet me the land-locked visitor
Come to her signal.

Certainly she looks rosy
– Far better than last spring
When she fell into the wind
Like a plinth of jetsam
And, defenceless and dumb,
In a three-day marathon
Was tried to death.
The judge was capped
But the jury had found prematurely;
There was an extra-sensory appeal
And a verdict conceded 'not proven'.

Certainly she is a different woman now
By some eerie fluke.
Cerebration has ceased
But, such is the mettle of the human system,
Means are extant to activate laughter
And the other channels are working.
A wide smile has been posted up from ear to ear,
Painstaking dressers have sleeked her hair
And her gay eyes, shining and all at sea
And having no notion of inadequacy

Or the impotence of reason,
Do not beg rescue of her land-locked daughter.

Death has been contained
With not a hope nor a prayer in her living head:
Is this a miracle?

ALL AT SEA (2)

Notice too this plausible lady,
This stylish tableau buoyed and watchful
On the sofa's poop.
These eyes firing their blank of welcome
Up from that comfortable deck
And lips posed for salute
Greet you, the land-locked visitor
Come to my signal.

Certainly I look rosy
– Far better than last year
When, three months into a marathon,
Unprepared, unruddered, undone,
I found I had self-destructed
And my happiness was gone.
But, on the verge of bedlam,
Sanity was saved by Morpheus
And never certifiably amok.
The ship righted
And sailed on . . .

Certainly I am a different woman now
By some eerie fluke.
Hope has capsized
But, such is the mettle of the human system,
Means are extant to activate laughter
And all channels are working.
A wide smile has been posted up from ear to ear
The body dressed in character
And my gay eyes, shining and all at sea,
Hiding their notion of inadequacy

And the impotence of reason,
Do not beg rescue of my land-locked friend.

Death has been contained
With not a hope nor a prayer in my living head.
Is this a miracle?

A GRAVE CONDITION

In the sinister dream
She was naked and head-first,
Heeled-in like a tree,
Her blonde hair rooting into dirt.
Sap leaked from eyes and nose –
Drops that steeped the hapless planting.
Arms and legs waved to bewildered crows
Left unreplete,
Who'd scented blood but found no meat.

Yet rousing now under a sky-blue lens
In bivouac mundane
The sun slanting,
She'll compute
That waking has only magnified her nightmare
And learn that larks are mute
As long as dawn breaks only
Through slats of despair.

So should she
Solicit lobotomy
From the tree-surgeon in the sky
Now that the golden days before the dream
Have reversed beyond time,
Or take a poisoned prick
To the worm in her mind,
An act so well-rehearsed?

WE HAVE BEEN ROBBED, FRIENDS

We have been robbed, friends!
Shortly, in the small hours;
But pointless here
To raise prints with powder
Or on all fours
Scan this kempt floor.
The doors turning on their jambs
Reveal all stowed as before,
Nothing indecorously spewed or torn,
No obscene signatures
Or scuffed seedlings in the border;
In good order
Silver and porcelain galore
And documents folded in their drawer
Like clean linen.

But friends, from our very midst
There has been a snatch.
One of our company,
Ensconced in a row of tended beds,
Was mending for the morrow
With nurses hovering like gardeners
When, flouting their vigilance,
A sneak-thief audaciously pre-opted dawn,
Sidled in, drew near him
And cut his soul out of his frame
Like an exhibit.

Friends, at the funeral
They will excavate or incinerate
To dispose of the shell

But the criminal with his loot
Has bolted up an Everest into thinnest air
Or sunk somewhere in quickest sands,
Swept past this age;
We shall never sight him from our plateau.
And now this irreparable outrage
Must somehow be explained
And entered with a graver
On his record.

UNDER THE PINE, ON THE PARQUET

Here I am, sitting
In a chair on a parquet field
Under a pine sky,
Searching my fingers
Through its threadbare frame
For strands of sense,
Gabbing at a stranger.
Flatteringly she hangs on the warm air
Her dark eyes deep as drains
Set in porcelain
(A beauty, this familiar creature),
Letting the slippery truisms
Negotiate locks to her brain.
But now the windows of her soul
Are glazed obscurely
And my nails tearing at the catch.

On almost any day
Light dapples her patchwork cells unevenly,
I can just touch her wits with my words
But then they skew sideways
Like a stroked puppy,
Moved but not enlightened.
Sometimes I search
When they are much too far away.

The matter of it is
Her jigsaw sense is disarranged;
I need to nudge the parts
Towards their proper places,
Feeling inexpertly and blindly

For the spaces,
But they jumble in the frame.

– Except on rare days
When her tangential selves converge
And I am the stooge,
Susceptible, suggestible,
Especially here under the pine
On the parquet
Clutching at straws.

HAVING BURIED A PRECIOUS EMBRYO ALIVE

Having buried a precious embryo alive
I mouthed a prayer over the planting.
It had burst from its natural berth
To be incarcerated in a small bevelled urn,
Earthed over and firmed beneath the brim.

But now from its mouth
A green messenger has stretched
And pierced the tilth.
I shall wait on its growing
And, when it is copious,
Tuck it in a friable bed.
From a wrinkled pellet it will burgeon
Into a burning bush –
An incredible metamorphosis,
Nature willing.

THE AUDIT

Until you allow
The price of ecstasy
Against the wince in its wake
Like an afterbirth
To follow;

Weigh peace alongside war
Seventh heaven with terra firma
Wine by water;
Try settling with the piper
From passion's exchequer
And burning in blood
Owe the price of a fire;

Over-balance your budget
In accounting for expenditure
And, overdrawn on the instalments,
Are committed for debt;

You may have won favour
And banked its future against old age,
Kissed on a balconied stage
Or been to Verona . . .

You will not have lent yourself
For investment over and over
In insatiable extravagance;
Earned all you have
And given all you earned,
More, and mortgaged your estate;
Not have laboured at fulfilment unpaid

Like some tramp's slave
Or genie of a lamp,
Toiling at stone with a heart like an axe
To make love.

ONE INTO TWO WILL GO

Don't threaten
'This is our last parting . . .'
Nor trap us in the error
Of linking us forever;
We should always be cleaving,
Closing and reweaving –
Slack the tiller and remember
We don't dispose the tides.

Our life leave full of partings
And returning
Loud with greeting,
Shores must be swept to keep them sweet,
Never parting means
We'll never meet.
Rather temporary veil and temporal kiss
Than an eternity of loving
In claustrophobic bliss.

GOD KNOWS

Something is caught
In the throat of summer,
In a red-hot vault
Burnt bare, prisoner,
Gutted wings
Flapping at air.

Despair after
Shall succour that dove
In the compassionate darkness
Outside love
For a winter's age,
A cool caged aeon,
To stanch and cure.

But yea though I come
Through the valley of shadow
And the healed test
My bird of woman
Never will dare
To expose its scarred bravado
Or its downy breast
In the light of a love again
To the breath of another dragon.

God knows that Passion Sunday
Is a day of rest.

TORREY CANYON, SHIP OF DEATH

For the day that I forgot to remember,
One year after my mother's death,
A blush raced through
The tripes of my intestines
Seeking to bury its burning face.
But the date was a false signal:
That self left early
The battery-brain leaked dry
Skull was bereft,
And the chance fact irrelevant
That her remains were cancelled
Twenty months late.
The signed certificate
Was an overdue receipt.

Twenty months earlier,
While creamy coasts were bombed black
By the broken tanker,
Her bedridden shape was shrinking:
My mother dying
As the invasive fluid congealed
And a black ribbon tightened round the coast.
The calamities seemed tuned:
A spontaneous opinion from headline and doctor
Of 'never the same after . . .'

Procedures and purges saved our sandy flanks
But would be no match
For the creeping silt in her wits

As it corroded and ate in.
A sou'westerly wind
Shook out its stinking blanket
In the teeth of my face:
'She is sick, she must die,' it said,
'Before the crude petroleum
Starts to fade'.
But there was no funeral.

Then I could not have borne to know
That her state of life was a dominion of death
And her long passing
Would be devoid of landmark and milestone
Until the verdict was carried out;
That gregarious soul
Walled up alone in some meantime fastness
Impermeable by life or death,
Just lightness and darkness.

By another compassion,
When it happened I could calmly accept
That the lady was for burning;
She was quite unreal,
Only a sacrificial doll
(Else how could the tongue
Which had glibly denied me, her sole scion,
Beneath those blatantly unblinking eyes
Have been her own?).
The body had let its room
To a maverick.

Later,
When something unseen tripped my vision,
When something unheard broached me,
When something unfelt impressed,
I knew she was positive again
In a different fashion.

PROVERB

Parent pride in babe of making
Moulden fine and smooth-tooled,
A filly daughter
Eyes as pure as holy water,
Cradled in a barque to flourish
Upon their affluent tide . . .
Comes before her pasty waking,
No sweet tastes will kisses bring
Where roses were.
And more beside:
When powdery pap turns off milk's tap
And fails to nourish
Full-blown curls must head for fall;
Nature will suck up spout of spot
For sun to blot and shrivel o'er.
For comfort, there's nowt here.

Bald bawling beetroot babby
Swathed in shabby swaddles soon
Out of flaming womb;
A cardigan of wrinkled skin
This crinkled chit has on
To parcel it, and no parental welcome . . .
But all those scarlet blushes are
For flushing ivory, dewy nectar in the flower,
Lily whitens, lily opens
And redness to the veins drains, powered sap,
Corrugations wane and flop to wrap

Plumping flesh fresh and flat,
Kinks but left for slant of guile
Or creasing smile,
Her shiny pate the sun's silk-lined obeisance mat.